THE
BEDROOM AND BOUDOIR.

BY

LADY BARKER.

ART AT HOME

LONDON:
MACMILLAN AND CO.
1878.

LONDON :
R. CLAY, SONS, AND TAYLOR,
BREAD STREET HILL, E.C.

PREFACE.

TOO much attention can scarcely be expended on our sleeping rooms in order that we may have them wholesome, convenient and cheerful. It is impossible to over-estimate the value of refreshing sleep to busy people, particularly to those who are obliged to do much brainwork. In the following pages will, we hope, be found many hints with regard to the sanitary as well as the ornamental treatment of the bedroom.

W. J. LOFTIE.

CONTENTS.

LIST OF ILLUSTRATIONS.

THE
BED-ROOM AND BOUDOIR.

CHAPTER I.

AN IDEAL BED-ROOM.—ITS WALLS.

T is only too easy to shock some people, and at the risk of shocking many of my readers at the outset, I must declare that very few bed-rooms are so built and furnished as to remain thoroughly *sweet*, fresh, and airy all through the night. This is not going so far as others however. Emerson repeats an assertion he once heard made by Thoreau, the American so-called "Stoic,"—whose senses by the way seem to have been preternaturally acute —that "by night every dwelling-house gives out a bad air, like a slaughter-house." As this need not be a necessary consequence of sleeping in a room, it remains to be discovered why one's first impulse on entering a bed-room in the morning

should either be to open the windows, or to wish
the windows were open. Every one knows how
often this is the case, not only in small, low, ill-
contrived houses in a town, but even in very
spacious dwellings, standing too amid all the
fragrant possibilities of the open country. It is a
very easy solution of the difficulty to say that we
ought always to sleep with our windows wide open.
The fact remains that many people cannot do so ;
it is a risk—nay, a certainty—of illness to some
very young children, to many old people, and to
nearly all invalids. In a large room the risk is
diminished, because there would be a greater
distance between the bed and window, or a space
for a sheltering screen. Now, in a small room,
where fresh air is still more essential and precious,
the chances are that the window might open directly on the bed, which would probably stand
in a draught between door and fireplace as well.

I take it for granted that every one understands
the enormous importance of having a fireplace in
each sleeping-room in an English house, for the
sake of the ventilation afforded by the chimney.
And even then a sharp watch must be kept on
the housemaid, who out of pure " cussedness "
(there is no other word for it) generally makes it
the serious business of her life to keep the iron
flap of the register stove shut down, and so to do

away entirely with one of the uses of the chimney. If it be impossible to have a fireplace in the sleeping-room, then a ventilator of some sort should be introduced. There is, I believe, a system in use in some of the wards of St. George's Hospital and in the schools under the control of the London School Board, known as Tobin's Patent. Ventilation is here secured by means of a tube or pipe communicating directly with the outer air, which can thus be brought from that side of the building on which the atmosphere is freshest. If report can be trusted, this system certainly appears to come nearer to what is wanted than any with which we are yet acquainted, for it introduces fresh air without producing a draught, and the supply of air can be regulated by a lid at the mouth of the pipe. A sort of double-star is often introduced in a pane of glass in the window, but this is somewhat costly, and it would not be difficult to find other simpler and more primitive methods, from a tin shaft or loosened brick in a wall, down to half a dozen large holes bored by an auger in the panel of the door, six or eight inches away from the top, though this is only advisable if the door opens upon a tolerably airy landing or passage. If it does not, then resort to some contrivance, as cheap as you please, in the outer wall leading

directly into the fresh air.   In most private houses
it is generally possible to arrange for those to whom
an open window at night is a forbidden luxury, that
they should sleep with their door open.   A curtain,
or screen, or even the open door itself will ensure
the privacy in which we all like to do our sleeping,
but there should then be some window open on
an upper landing, day and night, in all weathers.
Believe me, there are few nights, even in our
rigorous climate, where this would be an impossibility.   Of course common sense must be the
guide in laying down such rules.   No one would
willingly admit a fog or storm of driving wind
and rain into their house, but of a night when
the atmosphere is so exceptionally disturbed it is
sure to force its way in at every cranny, and
keep the rooms fresh and sweet without the
necessity of admitting a large body of air by an
open window.

Supposing then that the laws of ventilation
are understood and acted upon, and that certain
other sanitary rules are carried out which need
not be insisted upon here,—such as that no
soiled clothes shall ever, upon any pretence,
be kept in a bedroom,—then we come to the
next cause of want of freshness in a sleeping-room :—Old walls.   People do not half
enough realise, though it must be admitted

they understand a great deal more than they once did, how the emanations from the human body are attracted to the sides of the room and stick there. It is not a pretty or poetical idea, but it is unhappily a fact. So the only thing to be done is to provide ourselves with walls which will either wash or clean in some way, or are made originally of some material which neither attracts nor retains these minute particles.

Nothing can be at once cleaner or more wholesome than the beautiful wainscotted walls we sometimes see in the fine old country houses built in Queen Anne's reign. A bedroom of that date, if we except the bed itself, and the probable absence of all bathing conveniences, presented a nearly perfect combination of fresh air, spotless cleanliness, and stately and harmonious beauty to the eyes of an artist or the nose of a sanitary inspector. The lofty walls of panelled oak, dark and lustrous from age and the rubbing of many generations of strong-armed old-fashioned housemaids, were walls which could neither attract nor retain objectionable atoms, and ventilation was unconsciously secured by means of high narrow windows, three in a row, looking probably due south, and an open chimney-place, innocent of "register stoves" or any other contrivance for blocking up its wide throat. Such a room rises up clearly before the eyes of my mind, and I feel certain that I shall never forget the deliciously quaint and hideous Dutch tiles in the fireplace, nor the expressive tip of Ahasuerus' nose in the tile representing his final interview with Haman. How specially beautiful was the narrow carved ledge, far above one's head, which served as a mantelpiece, over which simpered a faded lady with low, square-cut boddice, her fat chin held well into the throat, and a rose in her pale, wan little hand. A dado ran round this room about five feet from the floor, and I used to be mean enough, constantly, to try if it was a dust-trap, but I never could find a speck. That was because the housemaid had been taught how to wipe dust off and carry it bodily away, not merely, as Miss Nightingale complains, to disturb it from the place where it had comfortably settled itself, and disperse it about the room.

But what I remember more vividly in this room than even its old-time beauty, was the thorough *conscientiousness* of every detail. The cornice might fairly claim to rank as a work of art, not only from its elaboration, but from its finish. The little square carved panels on each side of the chimney, serving as supports to the mantelpiece, held but one leaf or arabesque flourish apiece,

yet each corner was as sharply cut, each curve
as smoothly rounded, as though it had been
intended for closest scrutiny. The wood of neither
walls nor floors had warped nor shrunk in all
these years, and the low solid doors hung as
true, the windows opened as easily, as if it had
all been built yesterday. What do I say? built
yesterday? Let any of us begin to declare his experience of a new, modern house, and he will find
many to join in a doleful chorus of complaints
about unseasoned wood, ill-fitting joists, and hurried
contrivances to meet domestic ills, to say nothing
of the uncomfortable effects of "scamped" work
generally. In spite of our improved tools, and our
greater facilities for studying and copying good
designs, I am convinced that one reason why
we are going back in decorative taste to the
days of our great grandmothers is, that we
are worn out and wearied with the evanescent
nature of modern carpenter's and joiner's work—
to say nothing of our aroused perceptions of its
glaring faults of taste and tone. Unhappily we
cannot go back to those dear, clean, old oaken
walls. They would be quite out of the reach of
the majority of purses, and would be sure to
be imitated by some wretched sham planking
which might afford a shelter and breeding-place
for all kinds of creeping things. No; let those

who are fortunate enough to possess or acquire
these fine old walls treasure them and keep them
bright as their grandmothers did ; not *whitewash*
them, as actually has been done more than once
by way of "lightening" the room.   And who shall
say, after that, that the Goths have ever been
successfully driven back?

I dwell on the walls of the bedroom because
I believe them to be the most important from
a sanitary as well as from a decorative point of
view, and because there is really no excuse for
not being able to make them extremely pretty.
You may tint them in distemper of some delicate
colour, with harmoniously contrasting lines at the
ceiling, and so be able to afford to have them
fresh and clean as often as you choose, or you
may paint them in oils and have them washed
constantly.   But there is a general feeling against
this cold treatment of a room which, above all
others, should, in our capricious climate, be essentially warm and comfortable.   The tinted walls
are pretty when the curtains to go with them
are made of patternless cretonne of precisely the
same   shade,   manufactured   on   purpose,   with
exactly the same lines of colour for bordering.
I am not sure, however, that the walls I indi-
vidually prefer for a bed-room are not papered.
There are papers made expressly, which do not

attract dirt, and which can be found of lovely design. A bedroom paper ought never to have a distinct, spotted pattern on it, lest, if you are ill, it should incite you to count the designs or should "make faces at you." Rather let it be all of one soft tint, a pearly gray, a tender sea-shell pink, or a green which has no arsenic in it; but on this point great care is requisite. You should also make it your business to see, with your own eyes, that your new paper, whatever its pattern or price, is not hung *over* the old one, and that the walls have been thoroughly stripped, and washed, and dried again before it is put on.

Bedroom walls, covered with chintz, stretched tightly in panels, are exceedingly clean and pretty, but they must be arranged so as to allow of being easily taken down and cleaned. The prettiest walls I ever saw thus covered, were made of chintz, with a creamy background and tendrils of ivy of half a dozen shades of green and brown artfully blended, streaming down in graceful garlands and sprays towards a dado about four feet from the ground. It was a lofty room, and the curtains, screens, &c., were made to match, of chintz, with sprays of ivy, and a similar border. I know other bedroom walls where fluted white muslin is stretched over pink or blue silk (prettiest of all over an apple-green *batiste*). I dislike tapestry extremely for bedroom walls; the designs are generally of a grim and ghostly nature, and even if they represent simpering shepherds and shepherdesses, they are equally tiresome. There is a Japanese paper, sometimes used for curtains, which really looks more suitable and pretty when serving as wall-hangings in the bedrooms of a country house. I know a whole wing of "bachelors' quarters" papered by fluted Japanese curtains, and they are exceedingly pretty. The curtains of these rooms are of workhouse sheeting lined and bordered with Turkey red, and leave nothing to be desired for quaint simplicity and brightness. I must ease my mind by declaring here that I have a strong prejudice against Japanese paper except when used in this way for wall decoration. The curtains made of it are not only a sham, pretending to be something which they are not—a heinous crime in my eyes—but they are generally of very ugly patterns, and hang in stiff, ungraceful folds, crackling and rustling with every breath of air, besides being exceedingly inflammable.

Of course the first rule in bedroom decoration, as in all other, is that it should be suitable to the style of the house, and even to the situation in which the house finds itself. The great point in the wall-decoration of a town bedroom is that you should be able to replace it easily when it gets

dirty, as it is sure to do very soon if your windows
are kept sufficiently open. I *have* known people
who kept the windows of both bed and sitting-
rooms always shut for fear of soiling the walls.
I prefer walls, under such conditions, which can be
cheaply made clean again perpetually. There are
wall-papers by the score, artistically simple enough
to please a correct taste, and sufficiently cheap not
to perceptibly shrink the shallowest purse.

But in the country it is every one's own fault if
they have not a lovely bedroom. If it be low, then
let the paper be suitable—something which will
not dwarf the room. I know a rural bedroom with
a paper representing a trellis and Noisette roses
climbing over it; the carpet is shades of green without any pattern, and has only a narrow border
of Noisette roses; the bouquets, powdered on the
chintzes, match, and outside the window a spread-
ing bush of the same dear old-fashioned rose
blooms three parts of the year. That is a bower
indeed, as well as a bedroom. Noisette roses
and rosebuds half smothered in leaves have been
painted by the skilful fingers of the owner of
this room on the doorhandles and the tiles of the
fire-place as well as embroidered on the white
quilt and the green cover of the writing-table.
But then I acknowledge it is an exceptionally
pretty room to begin with, for the dressing-table

stands in a deep bay window, to which you ascend by a couple of steps. Belinda herself could not have desired a fairer shrine whereat to worship her own beauty.

The memory of other walls rises up before me; even of one with plain white satiny paper bordered by shaded pink ribbon, not merely the stiff paper-hanger's design, but cut out and fixed in its place by a pair of clever hands. This border of course looked different to anything else of the kind I had ever seen; but according to strict rules of modern taste it was not "correct." Yet a great deal depends on the way a thing is done. I see the Misses Garrett frowning as I go on to say that here and there a deep shadow was painted under it, and its bows and ends drooped down at the corners of the room, whilst over the fireplace they made the bright, circling border for a chalk drawing of a rosy child's head. But it *was* a pretty room, notwithstanding its original faulty design, and I describe it more as an illustration of the supremacy of a real genius for decoration over any hard and fast rule than as an example to be copied. Rules are made for people who cannot design for themselves, and original designs may be above rules, though they should never be above taste.

I might go on for ever describing bedroom walls instead of only insisting on their possessing the cardinal virtues of cleanliness and appropriateness. Whether of satin or silk, of muslin or chintz, or of cheapest paper, nothing can be really pretty and tasteful in wall decoration which is not scrupulously clean, without being cold and glaring, and it should be in harmony with even the view from the windows. Every room should possess an air of individuality—some distinctive features in decoration which would afford a clue to the designer's and owner's special tastes and fancies. How easy it is to people old rooms with the imaged likeness of those who have dwelt in them, and how difficult it would be to do as much for a modern bower!

. If I had my own way, I would accustom boys as well as girls to take a pride in making and keeping their bedrooms as pretty and original as possible. Boys might be encouraged to so arrange their collections of eggs, butterflies, beetles, and miscellaneous rubbish, as to combine some sort of decorative principle with this sort of portable property. And I would always take care that a boy's room was so furnished and fitted that he might feel free, there at least, from the trammels of good furniture. He should have bare boards with only a rug to stand on at the bed-side and fire-place, but he should be encouraged to make with his own hands picture-frames, bookcases, brackets, anything he liked, to adorn his room, and this room should be kept sacred to his sole use wherever and whenever it was possible to do so. Girls might also be helped to make and collect tasteful little odds and ends of ornamental work for their own rooms, and shown the difference between what is and is not artistically and intrinsically valuable, either for form or colour. It is also an excellent rule to establish that girls should keep their rooms neat and clean, dust their little treasures themselves, and tidy up their rooms before leaving them of a morning, so that the servant need only do the rougher work. Such habits are valuable in any condition of life. An eye so trained that disorder or dirt is hideous to it, and a pair of hands capable of making such conditions an impossibility in their immediate neighbourhood, need be no unworthy addition to the dowry of a princess.

CHAPTER II.

CARPETS AND DRAPERIES.

N the very old-fashioned, stately rooms of Queen Anne's reign the carpeting was doled out in small proportions, and a somewhat comfortless air must have prevailed where an expanse of floor was covered here and there by what we should now characterise as a shabby bit of carpeting. In fact a suitable floor-covering or appropriate draperies for these old rooms is rather a difficult point. Modern tastes demand comfort and brightness, and yet there is always the dread of too glaring contrasts, and an inharmonious groundwork. Quite lately I saw a fine old-time wainscotted room, whose walls and floor had taken a rich dark gloss from age, brightened immensely and harmoniously by four or five of those large Indian cotton rugs in dark blue and white, to be bought now-a-days cheaply enough in Regent

Street. The china in this room was of Delft ware, also blue and white, and it had *short* full curtains of a bright French stuff, wherein blue lines alternated with a rich red, hanging in the deep windows, whilst colour was given in a dusky corner by a silken screen of embroidered

peonies. A Turkish carpet is of course inadmissible in a bedroom, and the modern Persian rugs are too gaudy to harmonise well with the sober tone of a wainscotted bedroom, but it is quite possible to find delicious rugs and strips of carpeting in greenish blue copied from Eastern designs. The difficulty is perhaps most simply met by a carpet of a very dark red, with the smallest possible wave or suggestion of black in it, either in strips or in a square, stopping short within two feet or so of the walls, I know a suite of old-fashioned bedrooms where the floor is covered with quite an ecclesiastical-looking carpet, and it looks very suitable, warm and bright, and thoroughly in keeping. In a house of moderate size there is nothing I like so much as the whole of a bedroom floor being carpeted in the same way—landings, passages, dressing-rooms, and all—and on the whole, taking our dingy climate into consideration, a well-toned red carpet or nondescript blue will generally be found the most suitable.

Strange to say, next to red carpets white ones wear the best, but they make such a false and glaring effect, that they cannot be considered appropriate even for a pretty bowery bedroom, half dressing-room, half boudoir. With ordinarily fair wear white carpets only take a creamy tint as they get older, and then their bouquets and borders, have a chance of fading into better harmony. But most of the designs of these carpets are so radically wrong, so utterly objectionable from the beginning, that the best which can be hoped from time is that it will obliterate them altogether. It is true we flatter

ourselves that we have grown beyond the days
of enormous boughs and branches of exaggerated
leaves and blossoms daubed on a crude ground,
but *have* we escaped from the dominion of patterns, more minute it is true, but quite as much
outside the pale of good taste? What is to be said
in defence of a design which, when its colours are
fresh, is so shaded as to represent some billowy
and uneven surface, fastened at intervals by yellow
nails? or spots of white flowers or stars on a grass-
green ground? The only carpet of that sort of
white and green which I ever liked had tiny
sprays of white heather on a soft green ground, in
the miniature drawing-room of a Scotch shooting-
box. *There*, it was so appropriate, so thoroughly
in keeping with even the view out of the windows,
with the heathery chintz, the roe-deer's heads
on the panels of the wall, that it looked better
on the floor than anything else could possibly
have done. Morris has Kidderminster carpets for
bedrooms, in pale pink, buff, and blue, &c., which
are simply perfect in harmony of colour and
design.

People who consider themselves good managers
are very apt to turn the half worn-out drawing-
room carpet into one of the bedrooms, but this
is not a good plan, for it seldom matches the
draperies, and is also apt to become frowsy and

fusty. I am not so extravagant as to recommend that a good carpet with plenty of possibilities of wear yet in it should be thrown away because it is not suitable for a bedroom. There are many ways and means of disposing of such things, and even the threadbare remains of an originally good and costly carpet can find a market of its own. What I should like to see, especially in all London bedrooms, is a fresh, inexpensive carpet of unobtrusive colours, which can be constantly taken away and cleaned or renewed, rather than a more costly, rich-looking floor-covering, which will surely in time become and remain more or less dirty. But light carpets are seldom soft in tone, and I should be inclined to suggest felt as a groundwork, if the bare boards are inadmissible, with large rugs thrown down before the fireplace, dressing and writing-tables, &c. These should of course contrast harmoniously with the walls. If you have a room of which the style is a little too sombre, then lighten it and brighten it by all the means in your power. If it be inclined to be garish and glaring, then subdue it.

People cannot always create, as it were, the place in which they are obliged to live. One may find oneself placed in a habitation perfectly contrary to every principle of correct taste as well as opposed to one's individual preferences. But that

C 2

is such an opportunity! out of unpromising materials and surroundings you have to make a
room, whether bedroom or boudoir, which will
take the impression of your own state.   As long
as a woman possesses a pair of hands and
her work-basket, a little hammer and a few tin-
tacks, it is hard if she need live in a room which
is actually ugly.   I don't suppose any human
being except a gipsy has ever dwelt in so many
widely-apart lands as I have.   Some of these
homes have been in the infancy of civilisation, and
yet I have never found it necessary to endure, for
more than the first few days of my sojourn, anything in the least ugly or uncomfortable. Especially
pretty has my sleeping-room always been, though
it has sometimes looked out over the snowy peaks
of the Himalayas, at others, up a lovely New Zealand valley, or, in still earlier days, over a waving
West Indian "grass-piece."   But I may as well·
get out the map of the world at once, and try
to remember the various places to which my
wandering destiny has led me.   All the moral I
want to draw from this geographical digression is
that I can assert from my own experience—which
after all is the only true standpoint of assertion—
that it is possible to have really pretty, as well
as thoroughly comfortable dwelling-places even
though they may lie thousands of miles away from

the heart of civilisation, and hundreds of leagues
distant from a shop or store of any kind. I mean
this as an encouragement—not a boast.

Chintz is what naturally suggests itself to the
inquirer's mind as most suitable for the drapery of
a bedroom, and there is a great deal to be said in
its favour. First of all, its comparative cheapness
and the immense variety of its designs. Cretonnes
are comely too, if care be taken to avoid the very
gaudy ones. If there is no objection on the score
of difficulty of keeping clean, I am fond, in a
modern bedroom, of curtains all of one colour,
some soft, delicate tint of blue or rose, with a
great deal of patternless white muslin either over
it or beneath it as drapery to the window. This
leaves you more free for bright, effective bits of
colour for sofa, table-cover, &c., and the feeling of
the window curtains can be carried out again in
the screen. A bedroom, to be really comfortable,
should always have one or even two screens, if it
be large enough. They give a great air of comfort
to a room, and are exceedingly convenient as well
as pretty. The fashion of draped toilet tables is
passing away so rapidly that they cannot be depended upon for colour in a room, though we get
the advantage in other ways. So we must fall
back upon the old idea of embroidered quilts
once more to help with colour and tone in our

bedrooms. They are made in a hundred different
and almost equally pretty designs. Essentially
modern quilts for summer can be made of lace or
muslin over pink or blue batiste or silk to match
the tints of the room ; quilts of linen embroidered
with deliciously artistic bunches of fruit or flowers
at the edge and corners ; quilts of eider-down
covered with silk, for preference, or if our means
will not permit so costly a material, then of *one*
colour, such as Turkey red, in twilled cotton. I
have never liked those gay imitation Indian quilts.
They generally " swear " at everything else in the
room.

But there are still more beautiful quilts of an
older style and date. I have seen some made of
coarse linen, with a pattern running in parallel
strips four or six inches wide, formed by pulling
out the threads to make the groundwork of an
insertion. The same idea looks well also when
carried out in squares or a diamond-shaped pattern. Then there are lovely quilts of muslin
embroidered in delicate neutral tints, which look
as if they came straight from Cairo or Bagdad,
but which have never been out of England, and
owe their lightness and beauty to the looms of
Manchester.

One of the prettiest and simplest bedrooms I
know had its walls covered with lining paper of

the very tenderest tint of green, on which were hung some pretty pastel sketches, all in the same style. The chintzes, or rather cretonnes, were of a creamy white ground with bunches of lilacs powdered on them, and the carpet, of a soft green, had also a narrow border with bouquets of lilacs at each corner. The screens were of muslin over lilac batiste, and the quilt of the simple bedstead had been worked by the owner's own fingers, of linen drawn out in threads. The very tiles of the fireplace—for this pretty room had an open hearth with a sort of basket for a coal fire in the middle—and the china of the basin-stand as well as the door-handles and plates, were all decorated with the same flower, and although essentially a modern room in a modern house, it was exquisitely fresh and uncommon. This was partly owing to the liberal use of the leaves of the lilac, which are in form so exceedingly pretty.

In an old-fashioned house if I wanted the draperies and quilt of my bedroom to be thoroughly harmonious I should certainly go to the Royal School of Art Needlework in the Exhibition Road for designs, as they possess extraordinary facilities for getting at specimens of the best early English and French needlework, and they can imitate even the materials to perfection. I saw some curtains the other day

in a modern boudoir from this Royal School of
Art Needlework. They were of a delicate greenish blue silk-rep, which hung in delicious round
folds and had a bold and simple design of con-
ventionalised lilies in a material like Tussore silk
appliqué-d with a needlework edge. Of course they
were intended for a purely modern room, but there
were also some copies of draperies which went
beautifully with Chippendale chairs and lovely
old straight up and down cupboards and settees.

There is rather a tendency in the present day
to make both bedrooms and boudoirs gloomy; a
horrible vision of a room with walls the colour of
a robin's egg (dots and all) and *black* furniture, rises
up before me, and the owner of this apartment
could not be induced to brighten up her gloom by
so much as a gay pincushion. Now our grandmothers understood much better, though probably
no one ever said a word to them about it, how
necessary it was to light up dark recesses by contrasts. You would generally have found an exquisite old blue and white Delft jar full of scented
rose leaves, a gay beau-pot full of poppies, or even
a spinning-wheel with its creamy bundle of flax
or wool bound by a scarlet ribbon, in the un-
regarded corner of a dingy passage, and I think
we do not bear in mind enough how bright and
gay the costumes of those days used to be. To

a new house, furnished according to the present
rage for old-fashioned decoration, our modern
sombre apparel is no help. We do not lighten
up our rooms a bit now by our dress, except
perhaps in summer, but generally we sit, clad
in dingiest tints of woollen material, or in very
inartistic black silk, amid furniture which was
originally designed as a sort of background to
much gay and gallant clothing, to flowered sacques
and powdered heads, to bright steel buttons and
buckles and a thousand points of colour and light.
Let us follow their old good example thoroughly,
if we do it at all, and do our best to brighten the
dull nooks and corners which will creep into all
dwellings, by our attire, as well as in all other
ways.

CHAPTER III.

BEDS AND BEDDING.

HEN we discuss a bedroom, the bed ought certainly to be the first thing considered. Here at least, is a great improvement within even the last forty or fifty years. Where are now those awful four-posters, so often surmounted by huge wooden knobs or plumes of feathers, or which even offered hideously carved griffin's heads to superintend your slumbers? Gone, "quite gone," as children say. At first we ran as usual into the opposite extreme, and bestowed ourselves at night in frightful and vulgar frames of cast iron, ornamented with tawdry gilt or bronze scroll-work, but such things are seldom seen now, and even the cheap common iron or brass bedstead of the present day has at least the merit of simplicity. Its plain rails at foot and head are a vast improvement on the fantastic patterns of

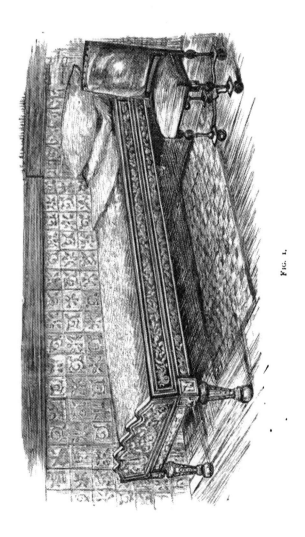

FIG. 1.

even twenty years ago, and the bedsteads of the present day will long continue in general use in modern houses. Their extreme cheapness and cleanliness are great points in their favour, and when they are made low, and have a spring frame with one rather thick mattress at the top, they are perfectly comfortable to sleep in besides being harmless to look at.

But in many rooms where the style of both decoration and furniture has been carried back for a century and a half, and all the severe and artistic lines of the tastes of those days must needs be preserved, then indeed an ordinary iron or brass bedstead, of ever so unobtrusive a pattern would be ludicrously out of place. Still, if our minds revolt from anything like a return to the old nightmare-haunted huge Beds of Ware, we can find something to sleep on which will be in harmony with the rest of the surroundings, and yet combine the modern needs of air and light with the old-fashioned strictness of form and beauty of detail. Here is a drawing (Fig. 1) made from an old Dutch bedstead by Mr. Lathrop. The sides are of beautifully and conscientiously inlaid work, whilst the slight outward slope of both the head and footboard insures the perfection of comfort. To avoid a too great austerity of form, the upper cap of the foot-board has been cut in curves, and the

solidity of the legs modified ever so slightly.
The bedding of this bedstead must by no means
project beyond its sides, but must fit into the

FIG. 2.

box-like cavity intended to receive it. In this
bedstead (Fig. 2), which was made from a design

by Mr. Sandier, more latitude is allowed in this
respect, and its perfect simplicity can only be
equalled by its beauty.

The form of wooden bedstead (Fig. 3), which
could easily be copied at all events in its general
idea, by any village carpenter, would be exceedingly pretty and original for a young girl's bedroom. It is intended to be of oak with side
rails which are to pass through carved posts,
and be held by wooden pins, as are also the
end rails. For durability as well as simplicity
this design leaves nothing to be desired, and it
can be made in almost any hard wood, whilst
every year would only add to its intrinsic worth.
How many of us mothers have taken special
delight in preparing a room for our daughters
when they return from school "for good"—
when they leave off learning lessons out of books,
and try, with varied success, to learn and apply
those harder lessons, which have to be learned
without either books or teachers.

What sumptuous room in after years ever affords
the deep delight of the sense of ownership which
attends the first awakening of a girl in a room of
her very own? and it is a vivid recollection of this
pure delight of one's own bygone girl-days which
prompts us to do our best to furbish up ever so
homely a room for our eldest daughter. If a

pretty, fresh carpet is unattainable, then let us have
bare boards, with rugs, or skins, or whatever is
available. Necessity developes ingenuity, and
ingenuity goes a long way. I never learned the
meaning of either word until I found myself very
far removed from shops, and forced to invent or

: Fig. 3.

substitute the materials wherewith to carry out my
own little decorative ideas.

Some very lofty rooms seem to require a more
furnished style of bed, and for these stately sleeping-places it may be well to have sweeping curtains of silk or satin gathered up quite or almost

at the ceiling, and falling in ample straight folds
on either side of a wide, low bedstead. They
would naturally be kept out of the way by slender
arms or brackets some six or eight feet from the
floor, which would prevent the curtains from
clinging too closely round the bed, and give the
right lines to the draperies. But, speaking indi-
vidually, it is never to such solemn sleeping-places
as these, that my fancy reverts when, weary
and travel-stained, and in view of some homely
wayside room, one thinks by way of contrast, of other and prettier bedrooms. No, it is
rather to simple, lovely little nests of chintz and
muslin, with roses inside and outside the wall,
with low chairs and writing table, sofa and toilet
all in the same room—a bedroom and bower in
one. Edgar Allan Poe declares that to

> " slumber aright
> You must sleep in just such a bed."

But he only says it of the last bed of all. Without
going so far as that, I can declare that I have
slumbered "aright" in extraordinary beds, in
extraordinary places, on tables, and under them
(that was to be out of the way of being walked
upon), on mats, on trunks, on all sorts of wonderful
contrivances. I slept once very soundly on a piece
of sacking stretched between two bullock trunks,
though my last waking thought was an uneasy

misgiving as to the durability of the frail-looking iron pins at each end of this yard of canvas, which fitted into corresponding eyelet holes in the trunks. I know the uneasiness of mattresses stuffed with chopped grass, and the lumpiness of those filled by amateur hands with wool—*au naturel.* Odours also are familiar unto me, the most objectionable being, perhaps, that arising from a feather bed in a Scotch inn, and from a seaweed mattress in an Irish hotel, in which I should imagine many curious specimens of marine zoology had been entombed by mistake.

But there is one thing I want to say most emphatically, and that is that I have met with greater dirt and discomfort, worse furniture, more comfortless beds (I will say nothing of the vileness of the food!), and a more general air of primitive barbarism in inns and lodgings in out-of-the-way places in Great Britain and Ireland, than I have ever come across in any colony. I know half-a-dozen places visited by heaps of tourists every year, within half-a-dozen hours' journey of London, which are *far* behind, in general comfort and convenience, most of the roadside inns either in New Zealand or Natal. It is very inexplicable why it should be so, but it is a fact. It is marvellous that there should often be such dirt and discomfort and general shabbiness and dinginess under circumstances which, compared with colonial difficulties, including want of money, would seem all that could be desired.

However, to return to the subject in hand. We will take it for granted that a point of equal importance with the form of the bedstead is its comfort but this must always be left to the decision of its occupant. Some people prefer beds and pillows of an adamantine hardness, others of a luxurious softness. Either extreme is bad, in my opinion. As a rule, however, I should have the mattresses for children's use *rather* hard—a firm horsehair on the top of a wool mattress, and children's pillows should *always* be low. Some people heap bedclothes over their sleeping children, but I am sure this is a bad plan. I would always take care that a child was quite warm enough, especially when it gets into bed of a winter's night, but after a good temperature has been established I would remove the extra wraps and accustom the child to sleep with light covering. A little flannel jacket for a young child who throws its arms outside the bedclothes is a good plan, and saves them from many a cough or cold. In the case of a delicate, chilly child, I would even recommend a flannel bed-gown or dressing-gown to sleep in in the depth of winter, for it saves a weight of clothes over them. I never use a quilt at night for children; it keeps in the heat too much, but blankets of the best possible quality are a great advantage. The cheap ones are heavy and not nearly so warm, whereas a good, expensive blanket not only wears twice as long, but is much more light and wholesome as a covering. Nor would I permit soft pillows; of course there is a medium between a fluff of down and a stone, and it is just a medium pillow I should recommend for young children and growing girls and boys. The fondest and fussiest parents do not always understand that, on the most careful attention to some such simple rules depend the straightness of their children's spines, the strength of their young elastic limbs, their freedom from colds and coughs, and in fact their general health. Often the daylight hours are weighted by a heavy mass of rules and regulations, but few consider that half of a young child's life should be spent in its bed. So that unless the atmosphere of the room they sleep in, the quality of the bed they lie on, and the texture of the clothes which cover them, are taken into consideration, it is only half their existence which is being cared for.

All bedsteads are healthier for being as low as possible; thus insuring a better circulation of air above the sleeper's face, and doing away with the untidy possibility of keeping boxes or carpet-bags

FIG 4

under the bedstead. There should be no valance
to any bedstead. In the daytime an ample quilt
thrown over the bedding will be quite drapery
enough, and at night it is just as well to have a
current of air beneath the frame of the bed. The
new spring mattresses are very nearly perfect as
regards the elasticity which is so necessary in a
couch, and they can be suited to all tastes by
having either soft or hard horsehair or finely picked
wool mattresses on the top of them. Whenever it
is possible, I would have children put to sleep in
separate bedsteads, even if they like to have them
close together as in Fig. 4.

There are many varieties of elastic mattresses,
though I prefer the more clumsy one of spiral
springs inclosed in a sort of frame. For transport
this is, however, very cumbrous, and in such a
case it would be well to seek other and lighter
kinds. It must be also remembered that these
spring mattresses are only suitable for modern
beds in modern rooms; the old carven beds of
a "Queen Anne" bedroom must needs be
made comfortable by hair and wool mattresses
only.

In many cases, however, where economy of
space and weight has to be considered, I would
recommend a new sort of elastic mattress which
can easily be affixed to any bedstead. It

resembles a coat of mail more than anything else and possesses the triple merit in these travelling days of being cool, clean, and portable.

The frowsy old feather bed of one's infancy has so completely gone out of favour that it is hardly necessary to place one more stone on the cairn of abuse already raised over it by doctors' and nurses' hands. A couple of thick mattresses, one of horsehair and one of wool, will make as soft and comfortable a bed as anyone need wish for.

Instead of curtains, which the modern form of bedstead renders incongruous and impossible, screens on either side of the bed are a much prettier and more healthy substitute. I like screens immensely; they insure privacy, they keep out the light if necessary, and are a great improvement to the look of any room. It is hardly necessary to say they should suit the style of its decoration. If you are arranging a lofty old-fashioned room, then let your screens be of old Dutch leather—of which beautiful fragments are to be found—with a ground-work which can only be described by paradoxes, for it is at once solid and light, sombre and gay. Any one who has seen those old stamped leather screens of a peculiar sea-green blue, with a raised dull gold arabesque design on them, will know what I mean. There are also beautiful old

Indian or Japan lacquered screens, light, and
with very little pattern on them ; even imitation

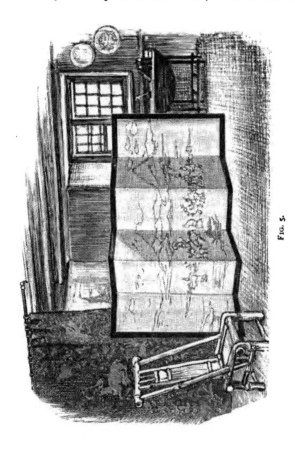

FIG. 5.

ones of Indian pattern paper are admissible to
narrow purses, but anything real is always much

more satisfactory. If again your bower is a modern Frenchified concern, then screen off its angles by *écrans* of gay tapestry or embroidered folding leaves, or paper-covered screens of delicate tints with sprays of trailing blossom, and here and there a bright-winged bird or butterfly. Designs for all these varieties of screens can be obtained in great perfection at the Royal School of Art Needlework. But for a simple modern English bedroom, snug as a bird's nest, and bright and fresh as a summer morning I should choose screens of slender wooden rails with fluted curtains of muslin and lace cunningly hung thereon. Only it must be remembered that these entail constant change, and require to be always exquisitely fresh and clean.

It often happens that another spare bed is wanted on an emergency, and it is a great point in designing couches for a nondescript room, a room which is some one person's peculiar private property, whether called a den or a study, a smoking-room or a boudoir, that the said couch should be able "a double debt to pay" on a pinch. I have lately seen two such resting-places which were both convenient and comfortable. The first was a long, low settee of cane, with a thin mattress over its seat, and a thicker one, doubled in two, forming a luxurious back against the wall by day. At night, this mattress could be laid flat out on the top of the other, which gave increased width as well as softness to the extempore bed.

The other, of modern carved oak, had been copied from the pattern of an old settle. It was low and wide, with only one deep well-stuffed mattress, round which an Algerine striped blue and white cotton cloth had been wrapped. Of course this could be removed at night, and the bed made up in the usual way. It struck me, with its low, strong railing round three sides, as peculiarly suitable for a change of couch for a sick child, though it could hardly be used by a full-grown person as a bed.

So now all has been said that need be on the point of a sleeping place. It is too essentially a matter of choice to allow of more than suggestion; and at least my readers will admit that I am only arbitrary on the points of fresh air and cleanliness.

CHAPTER IV.

WARDROBES AND CUPBOARDS.

OMETIMES a room has to play the part of both bedroom and boudoir, and then it is of importance what form the *"garde-robes"* shall assume. Fortunately there are few articles of furniture on which more lavish pains have been bestowed, and in which it is possible to find scope for a wider range of taste and choice. Recesses may be fitted up, if the room be a large one, and have deep depressions here and there in the masonry with doors to match the rest of the woodwork, panelled, grained, and painted exactly alike, and very commodious hanging cupboards may thus be formed. But however useful these may be to the lady's maid, they are scarcely æsthetic enough to be entitled to notice among descriptions of art furniture. Rather let us turn to this little wardrobe (Fig. 6), too narrow,

FIG. 6.

perhaps, for aught but a single gown of the present
day to hang in, yet exquisitely artistic and pleasant
to look upon. Its corner columns are mounted
with brass, and every detail of its construction is
finished as though by the hand of a jeweller. The
lower drawers are probably intended for lace or fur,
or some other necessary of a fine lady's toilette.
It is very evident from the accommodation provided
in the distant days when such wardrobes were
designed, that "little and good" used to be the
advice given to our grandmothers with their pin-
money, and that even in their wildest dreams they
never beheld the countless array of skirts and
polonaises and mantles and Heaven knows what
beside, that furnish forth a modern belle's equip-
ment. Yet these moderate-minded dames and
damsels must have loved the garments they did
possess very dearly, for the heroine of every poem
or romance of the last century is represented as
depending quite as much on her clothes in the
battle of life as any knight on his suit of Milan
mail. Clarissa Harlowe mingles tragic accounts of
Lovelace's villanies with her grievances about mis-
matched ruffles and tuckers, and even the excellent Miss Byron has by no means a soul above
court suits or French heels. Still these lovely
ladies had not much space assigned to them
wherein to bestow their finery when it was not on

their backs, and we must expect to find all the
wardrobe designs of former times of somewhat
skimpy proportions. Here is an antique lock-up
(Fig. 7) of French make (most of the best designs
for furniture came from France in those days) of a

FIG. 7.

very practical and good form to copy in a humbler
material. This is made of a costly wood, probably
rosewood, with beautifully engraved brass fittings
all over it. The door of the upper half seems

rather cumbrous, being only a flap which opens
out all in one piece, but a modern and less expensive copy might be improved by dividing this large
lid into a couple of doors to open in the middle

Fig. 8.

in the usual way, without at all departing from
the original lines.

Fig. 8, again, is more of a bureau, and affords
but scanty room for the ample stores of a lady's

B. R. E

lingerie. It is, however, of a very good design in its way, its chief value being the workmanship of its fine brass ornaments. The handles of the drawers are peculiarly beautiful, and represent the necks and heads of swans issuing from a wreath of leaves. It would look particularly well in a bedroom in a large old-fashioned country house, where the rest of the furniture is perhaps rather cumbrous as well as convenient, and the glitter of the metal mounting would help to brighten a dingy corner. It cannot, however, be depended upon to hold much, and is chiefly valuable in a decorative sense, or as a stand for a toilette glass.

In strong contrast to these two designs is Fig. 9 of modern Japanese manufacture. It is easy to see that the original idea must have been taken from a common portable chest of drawers, such as officers use. The slight alteration in its arrangement is owing to Japanese common sense and observation, for it would have required more strength of character than a cockney upholsterer possesses, to divide one of the parts so unequally as in this illustration. But the male heart will be sure to delight specially in that one deep drawer for shirts, and the shallow one at the top for collars, pockethandkerchiefs, neckties, and so forth. The lower drawers would hold a moderate supply of clothes, and the little closet contains three small drawers, besides a secret

place for money and valuables. When the two boxes,
for they are really little else, are placed side by
side they measure only three feet one inch long,
three feet four high, and one foot five deep. They

Fig. 9.

hardly appear, from the prominence of the sliding
handles, intended to be packed in outer wooden
cases as portable chests of drawers usually are;
but it must be remembered that in Japan they

E 2

would be carried from place to place slung on poles
carried on men's shoulders. There is a good deal
of iron used in the construction, which must be
intended to give strength, but it does not add to the
weight in any excessive degree, for it is very thin.
The wood is soft and light, and rather over-polished,
but the Japanese artist would have delighted in var-
nishing it still more, and covering it with grotesque
gilt designs in lacquer, if he had been allowed.
On page 55 will be found a roomy Chinese
cupboard with drawers and nicely-carved panels.

Many of our most beautiful old Indian chests of
drawers and cabinets have this black ground with
quaintest bronze or brazen clamps and hinges, locks
and handles, to give relief to the sombre groundwork. Except that the drawers seldom open
well, and are nearly always inconveniently small,
they are the most beautiful things in the world for
keeping clothes in, but it would certainly be as well
to have, out of the room in a passage, some more
commodious and commonplace receptacles. I have
seen a corridor leading to bedrooms, lined on each
side with wardrobes, about six or seven feet high,
consisting merely of a plain deal top with divisions
at intervals of some five feet from top to bottom.
A series of hanging cupboards was thus formed,
which had been lined with stretched brown holland,
furnished with innumerable pegs, and closed in by

doors of a neat framework of varnished deal with
panels of fluted chintz. Besides these doors to
each compartment, an ample curtain hung within,
of brown holland, suspended by rings on a slender
iron rod ; and this curtain effectually kept out all
dust and dirt, and preserved intact the delicate
fabrics within. Such an arrangement must have
been, I fear, far more satisfactory to the soul of
the lady's maid than the most beautiful old Indian
or French chest of drawers.

For rooms which are not old-fashioned in style,
and in which it is yet not possible to indulge in
French *consoles* or Indian cabinets as places to
keep clothes in, then I would recommend the
essentially modern simple style of wardrobe and
chest of drawers. I would eschew "gothic," or
"mediæval," or any other style, and I would avoid
painted lines as I would the plague. But there
are perfectly simple, inoffensive wardrobes to
be procured of varnished pine or even deal (and
the former wears the best) which, if it can only
be kept free from scratches, is at least in good
taste and harmony in a modern, commonplace
bedroom. It is quite possible, however by the
exercise of a little ingenuity to dispense with modern,
bought wardrobes, and to invent something which
will hold clothes, and yet be out of the beaten track.
I happened only the other day, to come across so

good an example of what I mean,[1] that I feel it ought to be described. First of all, it must be understood that the bedroom in question was a small one, in a London house recently decorated and fitted up in the style which prevailed in Queen Anne's reign, and to which there is now such a decided return of the public taste. The other portions of the furniture were in accordance with the original intention of the room and consisted of a very beautiful, though simple, carved oaken bedstead, and a plain spindle-legged toilette table and washstand, also old in design. The chairs were especially fine, having been bought in a cottage in Suffolk, and yet they matched the bedstead perfectly. They had substantial rush-bottomed seats, but the frame was of fine dark oak, and the front feet spread out in a firm, satisfactory fashion giving an idea of solidity and strength. The fireplace was tiled after the old style, and the mantelpiece consisted of a couple of narrow oak shelves, about a dozen inches apart, connected by small pillars. These ledges afforded a stand for a few curious little odds and ends, and on the top shelf stood some specimens of old china. But the difficulty remained about the wardrobe, for the room was too small to admit old *bureaus* which would only hold half a dozen articles of clothing.

[1] See Frontispiece.

So the ingenious owner devised a sort of corner
cupboard to fit into an angle of the room, and to
match the rest of the woodwork in colour and style,
having old brass handles and plates like those on

FIG. 10.

the doors. It is a sort of double cupboard ; that
is to say, whilst the left-hand side is a hanging
wardrobe which only projects away from the wall
sufficiently to allow the dresses to be hung up
properly, the right-hand division is a chest of

drawers.   Not a row of commonplace drawers,
however.   No ; the front surface is broken by the
introduction of little square doors and other
arrangements, for bonnets, &c.   We must bear in
mind these drawers extend much. higher than
usual, and the cornice being nearly on a level
with that of the wardrobe, there can be no
possibility of putting boxes and so forth on the
top; but then, on the other hand, a goodly range
of drawers of differing depth is provided.   It
certainly seemed to me an excellent way of
meeting the difficulty ; and I also noticed in other
bedrooms in the same house how odd nooks and
uneven recesses were filled in by a judicious
blending of cupboard and wardrobe which is evidently convenient in practice as well as exceedingly
quaint yet correct in theory.

CHAPTER V.

FIRE AND WATER.

ERHAPS the part of any room which is most often taken out of, or put beyond the decorative hands of its owner, is the fireplace. And yet, though it is one of the most salient features in any English dwelling, it is, nine cases out of ten, the most repulsively ugly. When one thinks either of the imitation marble mantelpiece, or its cotton velvet and of false-lace-bedizened shelves, the artistic soul cannot refrain from a shudder. The best which can be hoped from an ordinary modern builder is that he will put in harmless grates and mantelpieces, and abstain from showy designs. The fireplace in either bedroom or boudoir should not be too large, nor yet small enough to give an air of stinginess, out of proportion to everything else. Here are two (Figs. 11 and 14). The design of

each is as simple as possible, of plainest lines, but
with no pretence of elaborate sham splendour. Fig.
11 is of course only suitable for a small unassuming
room, but if the tiles were old Dutch ones and
the rest of the bedroom ware quaint blue and
white Delft, an effect of individuality and suit-
ability would be at once attained.   Such a fire-

place would look best
in a room with wall-
paper of warm neutral
tints of rather an old-
fashioned design, · and
I should like a nice
straight brass fender
in front of it almost
as flat as a kitchen
fender with delightful
possibilities of sociable
toe-toasting about it.

Fig. 11.

Such a one I came
across lately that had been "picked up" in the
far east of London.   It was about eighteen
inches high, of a most beautiful simple, flat, form
with a handsome twist or scroll dividing the design
into two parts.   Although blackened to disguise
by age and neglect at the time of its purchase, it
shone when I saw it, with that peculiar brilliant and
yet softened sheen which you never get except

in real old brass; a hue seldom if ever attained in modern brazen work however beautiful the design may be. This fender stood firmly—a great and especial merit in fenders—on two large, somewhat projecting, feet, and its cheerful reflections gave an air of brightness to the room at once.

There must always be plenty of room for the fire, and the actual grate should of course be so set as

Fig. 12.

to throw all the warmth into the room. Then, though it is rather a digression,—only I want to finish off the picture which rises up before me,—I would have a couple of chairs something like this (Fig. 12), and just such a table for a book or one's hair-brushes a little in front of these two chairs. And then what a gossip must needs ensue! Of course I would have a trivet on the fire, or before it. No bedroom can look really comfortable without a trivet and a kettle ; a brass kettle for preference, as squat and fat and shining as it is possible to procure. There are charming kettles to be found, copied from Dutch designs.

Instead of the ordinary wide low mantelpiece one sees in bedrooms, I am very fond of two narrower shelves over such a fireplace as this. They are perhaps best plain oak, divided and supported by little turned pillars, and if the top shelf has a ledge half way a few nice plates look especially well. But there are such pretty designs for mantelpieces now to be procured, that it would be a waste of time to describe any particular style, and most fireplaces are made on scientific principles of ventilation. Nor is it, I hope, necessary to reiterate the injunction about every part of the decoration and detail of a room, whether fixture or moveable, matching or suiting all the rest. In some instances contrast is the most harmonious arrangement one can arrive at, but this should not be a matter lightly taken in hand. A strong feeling is growing up in favour of the old-fashioned open fireplaces lined with tiles, and adapted to modern habits by a sort of iron basket on low feet in the centre, for coals. Excellent fires are made in this way, and I know many instances where the prettiest possible effect has been attained. In a country where wood is

cheap and plentiful, the basket for coals may
be done away with and the fuel kept in its place
by sturdy "dogs," for which many charming hints
have been handed down to us by our grandfathers.
Over the modern fireplace, even in a bedroom,
a mirror is generally placed, but I would not
advise it unless the room chanced to be so dingy
that every speck of light must be procured by
any means. Still less would I have recourse to
the usual stereotyped gilt-framed bit of looking
glass. In such a private den as we are talking
about, all sorts of little eccentricities might be
permitted to the decorator. I have seen a looking-
glass with a flat, narrow frame, beyond which
projected a sort of outer frame also flat, wherein
were mounted a series of pretty little water-colour
sketches, and another done in the same way with
photographs—only these were much more difficult
to manage artistically, and needed to be mounted
with a back-ground of greyish paper. For a
thoroughly modern room, small oval mirrors are
pretty, mounted on a wide margin of velvet with
sundry diminutive brackets and knobs and hooks
for the safe bestowal of pet little odds and ends
of china and glass, with here and there a quaint
old miniature or brooch among them. In old, *real*
old rooms anything of this sort would, however,
be an impossibility, for the mantelshelf would

probably be carried up far over the owner's head
who might think herself lucky if she could ever
reach, by standing on tip-toe, a candlestick off

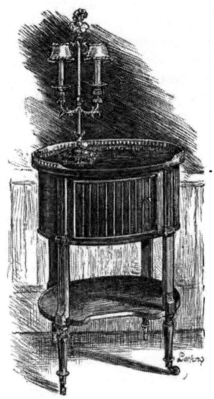

FIG. 13.

its narrow ledge. Our grandmothers seemed to
make it their practice to hang their less choice

portraits in the space above the mantelpiece, and
to this spot seem generally to have been relegated

FIG. 14.

the likenesses of disagreeable or disreputable, or, to
say the least, uninteresting members of the family ;

the successful belles and heroes occupying a more
prominent place downstairs. Fig. 14 shows a pretty
arrangement of picture, mirror and shelves for
china.

Before the subject of fire is laid aside, we must
just touch upon candles and lamps. Fig. 13 is a
simple and ordinary form of candlestick, which
would be safe enough from risk of fire if these
sheltering shades were made, as they often are,
of tin, painted green, and then there would be no
danger if it stood on a steady table, by the side of
even the sleepiest student. But perhaps this design
(Fig. 15) is the most uncommon, though it would
not be safe to put so unprotected a light except in
a perfectly safe draughtless place. However, there
is also in this branch of decorative art a great
variety of beautiful models to choose from. Antique
lamps, copied from those exquisite shapes which
seem to have been preserved for us in lava and
ashes during all these centuries, with their scissors
and pin and extinguisher, dangling from slender
chains, lamps where modern invention for oil and
wick meet and blend with chaste forms and lines
borrowed from the old designers, and where the
good of the eyesight is as much considered as
the pleasure to the eye itself.

Of washing arrangements, it is not possible to
speak in any arbitrary fashion. Here is a modern

French washing-stand (Fig. 16) made, however, to
close up, which is always an objectionable thing, in
my opinion, though it may often be a convenient one,
Let your basin invariably be as large as possible
and your jug of a convenient form, to hold and
pour from. Every basin-stand should be provided

Fig. 15.

with a smaller basin and jug, and allow at the same
time, plenty of space and accommodation for
sponges and soap. If, from dearth of attendance,
it is necessary to have a receptacle in the room, into
which the basin may be emptied occasionally
during the day, I would entreat that it should be
also of china, for the tin ones soon acquire an

P. R.   F

unpleasant smell even from soapsuds. But I detest
such contrivances, and they are absolutely inadmissible on any other score except economy of service.

Fig. 16.

All bathing arrangements would be better in a
separate room, but if this should be impossible,
then they should be behind a screen. But indeed

I prefer, wherever it is feasible, to contrive a small closet for all the washing apparatus, and to keep basin-stand, towel-horse, and bath in it.

It is sometimes difficult to hit exactly upon a plan for a washing-stand for a very small room or

FIG. 17.

corner, and a copy of this Chinese stand (Fig. 17) for a basin and washing appliances, would look very quaint and appropriate in such a situation. Only real, coarse, old Indian, or Japanese china, would go well with it, however, or it might be fitted with one of those wooden lacquered bowls from Siam,

F 2

FIG. 18.

and a water-jar from South America of fine red clay, and of a most artistic and delightful form. There are hundreds of such jars to be bought at Madeira for a shilling or two, and they keep water deliciously cool and fresh. If a demand arose for them they would probably be imported in large quantities. All washing-stands are the better for a piece of Indian matting hung at the back, for much necessary flirting and flipping of water goes on at such places, which stains and discolours the wall; but then this matting must constantly be renewed, for nothing can be more forlorn to the eye or unpleasing to the sense of smell, than damp straw is capable of becoming in course of time.

For the corner of a boy's bedroom, or for the washing apparatus of that very convenient little cupboard or closet or corner which I always struggle to institute *down*-stairs, close to where the gentlemen of the family hang their hats and coats, this (Fig. 18) is a very good design. It is simple in form and steady in build, and a long towel over a roller just behind it will be found useful. The towel need not be so coarse as the kitchen "round" one, from which it is copied ; and above all things do not have it *hard.* It is a needless addition to the unavoidable miseries of life to be obliged to dry your hands in a hurry on a new huckaback towel.

Many charming basin-stands have I seen extemporised out of even a shelf in a corner ; but such contrivances are perhaps too much of make-shifts to entitle them to mention here, only one hint would I give. Take care that your washing-stand is sufficiently low to enable you to use it with comfort. I once knew a very splendid and elaborate basin-stand, extending over the whole side of a dressing-room, which could only be approached by mounting three long low steps. I always felt thankful when my ablutions had ended and left my neck still unbroken.

CHAPTER VI.

THE TOILET.

HERE is no prettier object in either bedroom or boudoir than the spot where "the toilet stands displayed." Whether it be a shrine *à la Duchesse* (Fig. 19) or the simplest form of support for a mirror, it will probably be the most interesting spot in the room to its fair owner. Consequently there is nothing upon which the old love of decoration has more expended itself even from its earliest days, or which modern upholstery makes more its special study than this truly feminine shrine. I will say nothing of mirrors with three sides which represent you as a female "Cerberus, three ladies in one," or indeed of mirrors of any sort or kind, as our business lies at this moment more with the tables on which they should stand. These can be found or invented of every imaginable form, and contain

every conceivable convenience for receiving and
hiding away the weapons which beauty (or rather

FIG. 19.

would-be-beauty, which is not at all the same
thing) requires.

Here (Fig. 20) is a sort of old-fashioned *tiroir* of
an exquisite simplicity, and with but little space
outside for the " paraphernalia " of odds and ends

FIG. 20.

which the law generously recognises as the sole and
individual property of even a married woman.
Such articles would need to be stowed away in

one of its many drawers. Instead of the frivo-
lous drapery which would naturally cover a ·deal
toilet-table, the only fitting drapery for this

Fig. 21.

beautiful old piece of furniture (of French design
evidently) would be an embroidered and fringed
strip of fine linen which should hang low down on

either side. In a darksome room, imagine how the subdued brightness of its metal mountings would afford coigns of vantage to every stray sunbeam or flickering ray from taper or fire! And in its deep, commodious drawers too, might be neatly stowed away every detail of toilet necessaries. On it should stand a mirror which must imperatively be required to harmonise, set in a plain but agreeable frame without anything to mar the severe simplicity of the whole. There are several pieces of old furniture, however, which are better adapted to be used as toilet-tables than the subject of the illustration. Such a piece of furniture is more suitable when it is divided, as is often the case, into three compartments, the centre one being considerably further back than the side-pieces. In this way a place is secured for the knees, when seated at it, and this central cupboard, when filled with shelves, makes an excellent receptacle for brushes and combs, and so forth.

The defect of these old *tiroirs* is that they are rather small and low, and consequently look best in a small room, but they offer great variety of decorative embellishment (Fig. 21), and are very satisfactory, as stands for a small oval toilet-glass in an old frame to match. The designs too of the brass mountings for door and drawer are nearly always exceedingly beautiful, and vary from the simplest shining ring to a small miracle of artistic brazen work. These shining handles take away a good deal from the severity of decorative treatment which would naturally exist in the rest of the room, and it is under such conditions, where form takes precedence of colour, that we learn the full value of these little traps to attract and keep a warm glitter of light.

Here is a simpler design for a toilet-table (Fig. 22) which would look very well standing between the windows of a lofty room. If it was found that a good light for the looking-glass had been sacrificed to the general harmony of the room, then a smaller glass might be placed *in* a window, just for occasional use.

Some of the old-fashioned "toilet-equipages" are very beautiful just as they have come down to us. They are occasionally made in silver, and comprise many articles which cannot by any possibility be brought within the faith or practice of a modern belle. Still they offer charming forms for imitation, especially in the frames of the old hand-mirrors, whose elaborate simplicity (if one may use such a paradox) puts to shame the more ornate taste of their modern substitutes. Next to silver or tortoise-shell, I like ivory, as the material for a really beautiful and artistic set of toilet appendages, its delicious creamy tint going especially well with all shades of blue in a room. But I prefer the surface of the ivory kept plain and not grotesquely carved as you get it in China or Japan, for dust and dirt always take possession of the interstices, and lead to the things being consigned to a drawer. Now I cannot endure to possess any thing of any kind which had better be kept out of sight wrapped carefully away under lock and key. My idea of enjoying ownership is for my possession to be of such a nature that I can see it or use it every day—and all day long if I choose—so I shall not be found recommending anything which is "too bright and good for human nature's daily food." I have seen toilet-tables under difficulties, that is on board of real sea-going yachts, where it has been necessary to sink a little well into which each brush, box or tray securely fitted; and I have seen toilet-tables in Kafir-Land covered with common sixpenny cups and saucers, and shown as presenting a happy combination of use and ornament, strictly in conformity with " Engleez fasson."

But perhaps our business does not lie so much with these as with the ordinary dressing-table which is now more used in the modern shape of a convenient table with a scoop out of the middle, beneath which the knees can fit when you are seated at it, and with a couple of drawers on each side. This too is covered by a white *servictte* of

FIG. 22.

some sort, and supports a large toilet-glass of
equally uncompromising utility and convenience.
But however readily these good qualities may be
conceded to the modern toilet-table it is but an
uninteresting feature in an ideal bower. If the
room be an essentially modern one, and especially
if it be in the country, nothing affords a prettier
spot of colour in it, than the old-fashioned toilet-
table of deal covered with muslin draperies over
soft-hued muslin or batiste. Of course the carica-
ture of such an arrangement may be seen any day
in the fearful and detestable toilet-table with a
skimpy and coarse muslin flounce over a tight-
fitting skirt of glaring pink calico, but this is a
parody on the ample, convenient stand for toilet
necessaries, the draperies of which should be in
harmony with the other colours of the room. It
would need however to possess many changes of
raiment, in order that it may always be kept up to
the mark of spotless freshness. These draperies are
prettier of plain soft white muslin without spot or
figure of any kind, and may consist of two or three
layers, draped with all the artistic skill the construc-
tor thereof possesses. It is also an improvement, if
instead of only a hideous crackle of calico beneath,
there be a full flounce or petticoat of batiste which
would give colour and graceful folds together.
This is a very humble arrangement I know, but

it can be made as effective as if it cost pounds instead of pence. And this is one of the strong points in all hints on decoration, that they should be of so elastic a nature as to be capable of expansion under favourable circumstances, though not beyond the reach of extremely slender resources.

I do not recommend draped mirrors for modern toilet-tables on account of the danger from fire, and I like the style and frame of the looking-glass on the table to harmonise thoroughly with the rest of the furniture.

CHAPTER VII.

ODDS AND ENDS OF DECORATION.

IT seems a pity that sofas and chairs made of straw or bamboo should not be more used than they are. I mean, used as they come from the maker's hands, *not* painted or gilded, and becushioned and bedizened into hopeless vulgarity. They are only admissible *au naturel*, and should stand upon their own merits. Those we have as yet attempted to make in England are exceedingly weak and ugly compared with the same sort of thing from other countries. In Madeira, for instance, the chairs, baskets, and even tables, are very superior in strength and durability, as well as in correctness of outline, to those made in England; and when we go further off, to the East, we find a still greater improvement in furniture made of bamboo. Here is a chair (Fig. 23), of a pattern familiar to all travellers on the P. and O. boats, and whose acquaint-

ance I first made in Ceylon. It is essentially a
gentleman's chair, however, and as such is sinking·
into an honoured and happy old age in the dingy

FIG. 23.

recesses of a London smoking-room. Without
the side-wings, which serve equally for a table or
leg-rest, and with the seat elongated and slightly

B. R.   .   G

depressed, such a chair makes a delicious, cool
lounge for a lady's use in a verandah.

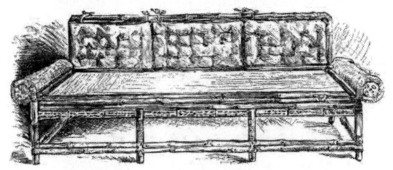

FIG. 24.

Then here (Fig. 24) is a Chinese sofa made of bamboo which, in its own country, would probably not be

FIG. 25A.

encumbered with cushions, for they can be removed

at pleasure. Where, however, there is no particular inducement to use cane or bamboo, then it
would be better to have made by the village carpenter a settee—or settle, which is the real word
—something like this. The form is, at all events
correct; and in a private sitting-room, furnished
and fitted to match, the effect would be a thousand
times better than the modern couches, which are
so often padded and stuffed into deformity.

Nothing can be simpler than the lines of the
design, as is seen in this drawing (Fig 25B), without

FIG. 25B.

the cushions; and it would come within the scope
of the most modest upholstering genius. In one's
own little den—which, by the way, I should *never*

G 2

myself dignify by the name of boudoir, a word
signifying a place to idle and sulk in, instead of

FIG. 26.

a retreat in which to be busy and comfortable—
such odds and ends of furniture, so long as there

FIG. 27.

be one distinct feeling running through it all, are far . more characteristic than commonplace sofas and chairs. If one *must* have large armchairs in a boudoir, or in a bedroom, here is one (Fig. 26) which is big enough in all conscience, and yet would go more harmoniously with an old-fashioned room than any fat and dumpy modern chair. If, on the other hand, the house in general, and this parti-cular room, chances to be essentially in the style of the present day, then you would naturally choose some of the comfortable modern easy-chairs, taking care to avoid the shapes which are a mass of padded and cushioned excrescences. But modern armchairs can be very pretty, and I know several which are low and long, and straight and unas-suming, and which yet preserve quite a good dis-tinct outline. Such chairs as these are a sort of half-way house between bed and board, between absolute rest and uncomplaining unrest; famous places for thinking, for watching, for chatting, and, above all, for dozing.

The bedrooms I am thinking of and writing about have, we must bear in mind, a certain element of the bower or boudoir or private sitting-room in them, and so I must stand excused for a suggestion about a place for books or music. Here is a delightful corner for a piano (Fig. 27), but sometimes such a thing is out of the question, and it is only possible to find space for a few shelves. These can always be made suitable and pretty either of a simple old form in plainest oak to

FIG. 28.

match the severe lines of an old-fashioned room, or of deal painted black, varnished, with a gilt line grooved in front, and a bit of bright leather to go

with a more modern room. To my mind books
are always the best ornaments in any room, and
I never feel at home in any place until my
beloved and often shabby old friends are un-
packed and ranged in their recess. I once
extemporised a capital book case out of a blocked-
up window, and with a tiny scrap of looking-
glass let in where the arch of the window
began its spring, and filled by some old bowls
of coarse but capital old china, whose gaudy
colours could only be looked at safely from a
distance.

As time goes on, one is sure, in such a beloved
little den, to accumulate a great deal of rubbish
dear, perhaps, only to the owner for the sake of
association. Which of us has not, at some tender
time of our lives, regarded a withered flower, or
valueless pebble, as our great earthly treasure?
So, in later days, a plate, a cup, a pipe will be
precious, perhaps, to one as mementoes of the
place and companions where and with whom it
was bought. But if such trifles, though too dear to
be laid aside, are yet not intrinsically good enough
to form part of a collection, and to take a prominent share in decoration, then I would either
stand them aside on a little *étagère* like that to
be found on page 79, or else get the carpenter
to put up graduated shelves, which may be quite

pure and simple in taste and yet suit the rest of
the room.   This (Fig. 28) is a capital valuable hint
to keep photographs or prints at hand, and yet in
safety.   Take my advice, and don't have fringe
or mock lace, or gilt nails at the edges by way of
decoration.   Have a nice piece of wood, walnut,
oak, even varnished pine, if you choose, neatly
finished off at the edge, or, if it suits the rest of
the room, black, with a little narrow gilt line in a
depression.   I think something ingenious might
be done with Japanese tea-trays, taking care to
choose good designs.

The worst of such a dear delightful den as I
am imagining, or rather describing, is the tendency
of the most incongruous possessions to accumulate
themselves in it as time goes on.   What do you
think of a pitcher like this (Fig. 29) standing in one
corner, just because, though of common ware, and
rather coarsely modelled, the colour of the earthen-
ware is delicious in tone, and the design bold and
free?   It was brought from South America, and
cost only six shillings, or thereabouts, but if it had
cost as many pounds it could not have been more
thoroughly in harmony with the surroundings of
its new home.

One hint may not be out of place here, and that
is with respect to table-covers.   Many people are
fond of covering up writing tables, and every occa-

sional table, with a cloth ; and these draped tables
are generally great eyesores in an ill-arranged
room. The covers seldom harmonise, and nowa-
days many hideous pieces of work are accom-
plished in the name of the School of Art which

Fig. 29.

are far removed from the artistic and beautiful
designs which alone proceed from the School itself.
There indeed you may find patterns which would
go beautifully with any old-time furniture, and
which might be worked on deliciously neutral tints
of cloth or serge. But beware of staring, gaudy

table-covers, of shabby material, of which the best
that can be hoped is that they may speedily fade
into better harmony. The Queen Anne tables
were never intended by their designer to be covered
up by drapery. They are generally inlaid in delicate designs, which it would be a sin to conceal;
nor could we afford to lose the slender grace of
the legs. The clumsy, ill-finished cheap table of
the present day is all the better for a cover, and
wonders may be done in improving a bare, cold,
unhappy-looking room, by a good table-cover here
and there, or a nicely embroidered sofa-pillow of
cloth or satin, or, better still, one of those lovely
new low screens, with the tall tufts of grass or
lilies which we owe to Walter Crane's skilful
pencil.

I confess I like a room to look as if it were
inhabited, and that is the only drawback that the
rooms furnished in the seventeenth century style
have in my eyes. You scarcely ever feel as if
any one lived in them—there are seldom any signs
of occupation, especially feminine occupation, lying
about, no "litter," in fact; litter being a powerful
weapon in the hands of a person who knows how
to make a room look comfortable. Then I am
told that litter is incongruous in a Queen-Anne
room, for that the women of those days had not
the same modes of employment as ourselves. The

greatest ladies, if they were blessed with an
energetic temperament, only gave it free scope
with their medicine chest or in their still-room or
linen closet; while the lazy ones were obliged to
dawdle away a good deal of their time in bed
or at their elaborate toilettes.   But still I am
always longing to overlay a little of the modish
primness of the distant days we are now copying,
with something of this busy nineteenth century's
tokens of a love of art or literature.   And in a
room with any claim to a distinct individuality of
its own, this would always be the case.

CHAPTER VIII.

THE SICK-ROOM.

OWEVER skilfully designed the arrangements of a house may appear to be, however sumptuously decorated and furnished its rooms, it is impossible to know whether a great law of common sense and practical usefulness has guided such arrangements, until there has been an illness in the house. Then will it be discovered—too late alas!—whether doors and windows open conveniently, whether fireplaces give out proper warmth, how the apparatus for ventilation works, and whether the staircases, landings, cupboards, and a thousand unconsidered items of the architect's labours have been planned in the best possible way, or in the stupidest. For the comfort and convenience of the patient at such times, it is by no means necessary that much money should have been spent on the construction of the house that chances to shelter him in his hour, of suffering, nor that its furnitures or decorations should be of a costly character. Fortunately such things need not aim at anything higher than cleanliness and convenience, and we only require to exert our own recollections in support of this assertion. As far as my individual experience goes, I have seen an old woman, who had been bed-ridden for years, more comfortably housed and tended beneath a cottage roof, and her room kept more exquisitely clean and sweet than that of many wealthy patients in splendid houses. Of course everything depends on the capacity for organisation and arrangement in the person who has charge of the invalid, but the nurse's task may be made much easier by having to perform it in a bedroom and under conditions which are in accordance with the exigencies of such a time.

Many smart and pretty-looking bedrooms are discovered by their sick owner to be very different abodes to what they seemed to him in health. Awkwardly-placed doors and windows produce unsuspected draughts; the too close proximity of an ill-arranged staircase or housemaid's closet becomes a serious trouble, and a low pitched ceiling prevents proper ventilation. It is more difficult than one imagines to find in a badly proportioned room a single convenient place for the patient's bed. It must be either close to the door, or touching the fireplace, or under a window or in some situation where it distinctly ought *not* to be. I have known such faults—faults which occasioned discomfort every moment, and had to be remedied by a thousand make-shift contrivances, occur in splendid rooms in magnificent houses; and I have known poor little modern dwellings in a colony to be perfectly free from them. When I am told, "such or such a room or house is a very comfortable one *to be ill in*," then I know that the construction and arrangement of that abode, however simple it may appear, must needs be up to a very high mark indeed. Of course a great deal can be done to modify existing evils, by a judicious arrangement of screens and curtains, by taking out useless furniture, by substituting a comfortable low bed, easy to get at, for a cumbrous couch where the unhappy patient's nose seems as if it was intended to rub against the ceiling, and various other improvements. But what can remedy a smoky chimney, or a grate where all the heat goes up the chimney, or windows that rattle, and doors that open in every direction except the right one? How can an outside landing or lobby be created at a moment's notice, or a staircase moved a yard further off? Of course if an illness gave notice before it seized its victim, if people ever realised that a house should be so constructed as to reduce the chances of illness to a minimum, and raise its possible comforts to a maximum if it did come, then everything would go on quite smoothly and we should certainly live, and probably die, happy. But this is exactly what we do not do, and this chapter would never have been written if I had not seen with my own eyes innumerable instances where neither want of money, nor space, nor opportunity for improvement were the causes of a wretchedly uncomfortable sick-room.

I have known bedrooms which looked nests of rosy, luxurious comfort until their owner fell ill, and then turned suddenly, as it seemed, into miserable comfortless abodes of frippery and useless, tasteless finery—where a candle could scarcely be placed anywhere without risk of fire, and where the patient has deeply complained of the way the decorations of the room " worried " her. As a rule, in a severe illness, sick people detest anything like a confusion or profusion of ornaments or furniture. If I am in authority in such a case, I turn all gimcracks bodily out, substituting the plainest articles of furniture to be found in the house. Very few ornaments are allowable in a sick-room, and I only encourage those which are of a simple, correct form. I have known the

greatest relief expressed by a patient, who seemed
too ill to notice any such change, at the substitu-
tion of one single, simple classical vase for a whole
shelf-full of tawdry French china ornaments, and
I date the recovery of another from the moment
of the removal out of his sight of an exceedingly
smart modern dressing-table, with many bows of
ribbon and flounces of lace and muslin. I do not
mean to say that the furniture of a sick-room
need be ugly—only that it should be simple and
not too much of it. Nothing confuses and worries
a person who is ill like seeing his attendants
threading their way through mazes of chairs and
sofas and tables; but he will gladly look and
find relief and even a weary kind of pleasure in
gazing at a table of a beautiful, simple form, placed
where it is no fatigue for him to look at it, with
a glass of flowers, a terra-cotta vase, a casket, anything which is so intrinsically beautiful in form as
to afford repose to the eye.

I have often observed that when people begin
to take pleasure in *colour*, it is a sure sign of
convalescence—for in severe illness, unless indeed
it be of such a nature as to preclude all power
of observation, form is of more importance to the
patient than colour. One learns a great deal
from what people tell one *after* they are well
enough to talk of such things as past, distem-

pered fancies. For instance, I was once nursing a typhoid fever patient, who lay for some
days in an agony of weakness. He had been deaf
as well as speechless, and all his senses appeared
to have faded away to the very brink of extinction.
Yet afterwards when he became able to talk of
his sensations at different stages of his illness, he
mentioned that particular time, and I found he
had been keenly conscious of the *forms* of the
objects around. He spoke of the pleasure which
the folds of a curtain had afforded him, of the
"comfort" of the shape of the old-fashioned
arm-chair in which I used to sit, and of how
grateful he had felt when he observed that
divers gimcracks had been removed from his
sight. Later, as he grew better, and the weary
eyes craved for colour, I found it necessary to
pretend to be busy dressing dolls or making
pincushions, to afford myself an excuse for a
little heap of brightest coloured silks and fragments of ribbon placed where he could see them,
and the daily fresh bunches of flowers were a
perpetual delight to his eyes.

An ideal sick-room then should first of all
possess walls which will not weary or worry the
sick person, and no *good* pattern will do this.
The low bed should be so placed that whilst it
would be sheltered from draught (the aid of one or

two screens will be useful here) the light would
not fall disagreeably on the patient's eyes. No
rule can be given about light. In some cases the
sick person loves to look out of the window all
day, whilst in others a ray of light *on* the face
is agony. In such circumstances the bed should,
if possible, be so arranged as to allow the light
to come from behind, for it is only in rare and
exceptional cases that sunshine as well as outer
air may not be admitted daily into a sick-room.
We are fast getting beyond the ignorance of a
north aspect for a bedroom, and most of us know
that sunshine is quite as necessary to a bedroom
as to a garden. No children will ever thrive
unless they have plenty of sunshine, as well as
air in the rooms in which they sleep, and a sick-
room should also have both in abundance. If the
weather be hot, it is easy, in England, to modify
the temperature by means of outer blinds, *per-
siennes,* open doors, and other means. Few people
understand what I have learnt in tropical countries, and that is, how to exclude the outer air
during the hot hours of the day. The windows of
the nursery or sick-room (for we all need to be
treated like children when we are ill) should be
opened wide during the early cool, morning-tide,
and the room flooded with sun and outer air.
Then, by nine or ten o'clock, shut up rigorously

every window, darkening those on which the sun would beat, *out-side* the glass—by means of blinds or outer shutters—until the evening, when they may all be set wide open again. All woollen draperies, curtains and valences should be done away with in a sick-room. If the windows are unsightly without curtains, and the illness is likely to be a long one, then substitute soft, patternless muslin or chintz, or, prettiest of all, white dimity with a gay border, but let there be no places of concealment in a sick-room. Every thing unsightly or inodorous should be kept out of it, and herein is found the convenience of a well-planned and well-arranged house, where clothes-baskets, and things of that sort, can be so bestowed as to be at the same time handy and yet out of the way.

If it were not for the unconceivable untidiness and want of observation which exists in the human race, such cautions as not to leave about the room the clothes the sick person has last worn, hanging up or huddled on a chair in a corner, would seem superfluous. But I have actually seen a girl stricken down by a sudden fever, lying at death's door, on her little white bed, whilst the wreath she wore at the ball where she took the fatal chill, still hung on her toilette glass, and her poor little satin shoes were scattered about the room.

She had been ill for days; there were two ladies'-maids in the house, besides anxious sisters, parents, and nurses, and yet no one had thought of putting these things out of sight. The first rule, therefore, to be observed in nursing even bad colds, where the sufferer may have to stay in bed a few days, is to send all the linen he has been wearing to the wash *at once*, and to put away everything else in its proper place. Boots should never be allowed in a sick-room, for the leather and blacking is apt to smell disagreeably and they ought immediately to be removed to another place.

Then there should be if possible *outside* the door of the sick-room, either on a landing or in another room, a convenient table, covered with a clean, white cloth, on which should be ranged spare spoons, tumblers, glasses, and so forth, and whatever cooling drinks are wanted, all so managed that dust shall be an impossibility. Inside the room, on another small table, or shelf, or top of chest of drawers, according to circumstances, should be kept also on a snowy cloth, just whatever is actually needed at a moment's notice—medicines and their proper glasses, &c., and a spoon or two, but the instant anything is used, it should be an established rule that the nurse puts the spoon or glass *outside*, and supplies its place with a clean one. In most cases, a servant need only renew the supply outside twice a day.

As for keeping trays with nourishment in the room, it is a sign of such careless nursing that I should hardly dare to mention it, if I had not more than once gone to relieve guard in a friend's splendid sick-room at daylight, and seen the nurse's supper-tray of the night before *on the floor* whilst the room, in spite of all its beautiful decorations, smelt sickly and disgusting with the odour of stale beer and pickles. It is incredible that such things should happen, but in the confusion caused by a sudden and severe illness, untidy and careless habits are apt to come to the surface, and loom largely as aggressive faults. Sickness is not only a great test of the sufferer's own character and disposition, but of those of the people around him, and as a general rule, I have discovered more beautiful qualities in sick people, and those about them, who dwell in cottages or even hovels, than in more splendid homes. Everyone knows how really kind poor people are to each other, and never more so than when the angel of disease or death is hovering over the humble roof-tree.

Food, or nourishment as it is called in sickroom phraseology, would not so often be refused by the patient if it were properly managed. Who does not know the wearisomeness of being asked, probably in the morning, when the very thought of food is an untold aggravation to one's sufferings what one could "fancy"? And this is probably followed by a discussion on the merits or possibilities of divers condiments, to each of which as it is canvassed before him the wretched patient is sure to declare a deep-rooted repugnance. A sick person, until he reaches that happy stage of convalescence when it is an amusement to him, should never be allowed to hear the slightest discussion on the subject of his nourishment. Whatever the doctor orders should be prepared with as wide a range of variety as can be managed, and offered to him in the smallest permissible quantities, exactly cold or hot enough to take, and served as prettily and daintily as possible, at exactly the right moment. The chances are a hundred to one that, if it is within the range of possibilities that he can swallow at all, he will take it. If he does not, there should be no argument, no attempt at forcing it on him ; it should at once be taken quite away and something different brought as soon afterwards as is prudent. Few people realise how extraordinarily keen the sense of smell becomes in illness, and how the faint ghost of a possible appetite may be turned into absolute loathing by the smell of a cup of beef-tea, cooling by the bed-side for ten minutes before it is offered.

I am always guided in a great degree about nourishment by the instincts of my patient, and I never force stimulants, or anything equally distasteful on a sick person who is at all reasonable upon such matters. I once had a patient to nurse, whose desperate illness had brought him very near the shadowy land. It had left him, and the doctors assured me that his life depended on how much brandy I could get down his throat during the night. I told him this, for he was quite sensible, when he refused the first teaspoonful, and he whispered in gasps, " I'll take as much milk as you like ; that stuff kills me." So I gave him teaspoonfuls of pure milk all through the night every five minutes, and not a drop of brandy. The doctor's first reproachful glance in the morning was at the untouched brandy bottle, and he shook his head, but when he had felt the sick man's pulse his countenance brightened, and he graciously gave me permission to go on with the milk. Of course there are cases when the patient never expresses an opinion one way or other, and then the only safe rule is to obey the doctor's orders, but I never fly in the face of any strong instinct of a sick person rationally expressed.

So now I hope we have some glimmering idea
of what a sick-room should be: cool in summer,
warm in winter, but deliciously sweet and fresh
and fragrant always. Simple in its furniture, but
the few needful articles, of as agreeable shapes
and as convenient as possible—a room which
can be looked back upon with a sort of affec-
tion as a place of calm, of discipline, and of
organization, as well as of the mere kindness
and willingness to help, which is seldom, if ever,
absent from a sick-room, but which is not the
beginning and end of what is necessary within
its walls.

There are bed-rests and bed-tables to be
hired for a sick person's use in almost any town
in England; or, if it is preferred, any village
carpenter could make a table with legs six or
eight inches high, and a top of a couple of smooth
light planks, about two feet six long, scooped
out in the middle. This is very convenient when
the patient is well enough to sit up in bed and
employ himself. The bed-rests are equally simple,
the upper half of a chair, padded, and made
to lower at convenience, while a loose jacket or
wrapper, easy to slip on, of flannel, should also
be provided to throw over the patient's shoulders
when he uses chair and table. When the patient
can sit up and occupy himself this sort of table

will be found a great comfort. It might just as
well be used when lying on a sofa.

One word more, like a postscript, for it has no
real business to intrude itself here. It is only an

Fig. 30.

entreaty to all nurses or those in authority in a
sick-room, to wear the prettiest clothes they
possess. Not the smartest, far from it; the
simplest cottons, cambrics, what you will, but nice
and fresh and pleasant to look at. If it is only a

dressing-gown it may be a charming one. No hanging sleeves, or dangling chains, or streaming ribbons, but sufficient colour for weary eyes to rest on with pleasure. An ideal toilette for sick room nursing would be a plain holland or cambric gown, made with absolute simplicity—long enough to be graceful without possessing a useless train —rather tight sleeves, and no frills or furbelows ; a knot of colour at the throat and in the hair, or on the cap—only let your ribbons be exquisitely fresh and clean—and a nice large apron, or rather bib, with one big pocket in front. This apron may be tied back—not too tightly, please—with the same coloured ribbons, and a little change of hue now and then is a great rest and refreshment in a sick room. There are charming linen aprons now embroidered in School of Art designs of the shape I allude to, but they can be made equally well in print, or plain holland, or linen.

No garment that rustles or creaks, or makes its presence audible should ever cross the threshold, but the toilette of the nurse should always be exquisitely clean and neat, and yet as bright and pretty as possible. No sitting up at night, no anxiety or unhappiness should be an excuse for a dirty, dishevelled attendant in a sick-room. It is *always* possible to steal half an hour morning and evening to wash and change, and do one's hair neatly, and the gain and comfort to the patient as well as to the nurse, is incalculable. This also would not be touched upon if my own recollections did not supply me with so many instances, where all this sort of care was considered to be absolutely worthless, and yet sick people have remarked afterwards how perfectly conscious they had been of all such shortcomings, and how such and such a tumbled cap, or shawl pinned on awry had been like a nightmare to them. Beauty itself is never more valuable than in a sick-room, and if laws could be passed on the subject, I should like to oblige all the pretty girls of my acquaintance to take it in turn to do a little nursing. I venture to say that no ball-room triumphs would ever compare with the delight their possession of God's greatest and best gift would afford to His sick and suffering creatures. But a nurse may always make herself look pleasant and agreeable, and if she have the true nursing instinct, the ready tact and sympathy which a sick-bed needs, she may come to be regarded as "better than pretty" by her grateful patient.

CHAPTER IX.

THE SPARE ROOM.

ERHAPS the kindliest and wisest advice with regard to a spare room, would be the same as *Punch's* famous counsel to young people about to marry—a short and emphatic "Don't." In a large country house, perhaps even in a small country house, the case is different, for the spare room too often represents all the social variety which the owners can hope for, from year's end to year's end—and the only change from town life possible to half the bees in the great hive. It is scarcely possible to imagine an English country house, be it ever so humble, without its spare room, or the warm cordial welcome which would be sure to greet its succeeding inhabitants. How fresh and sweet and dainty do its simple appointments look to jaded eyes! how grateful its deep stillness to world-deafened ears! How impossible, in a brief summer

week, to believe that life can ever be found dull
or monotonous amid such delicious calm! A
walk in the gloaming in a country lane,—always
supposing it is not too muddy—a cup of milk
fresh from the cow, a crust off the home-baked loaf,
are all treats of the first order to the tired cockney.
I have often noticed the sort of half-pitying, half-
contemptuous amazement with which my country
hostess has beheld my delight at being installed
in her spare room, my rapture at the sight of
meadows and trees, or the sound of cawing rooks
and the whirr of mowing machines. And how
fresh and clean ought this country spare room to
look! How inexcusable would be stain or spot,
or evil odour amid such fragrant surroundings!
Why should not the sheets *always* smell of lavender
(as a matter of fact, they do not, I regret to state)?
why should not there be *always* a jar of dried
rose-leaves somewhere "around," as our dear,
epigrammatic, Yankee cousins say?

I do not think I really like silks and satins
anywhere; I acknowledge that they fill me
with a respectful admiration and awe for a
short space, but that soon wears off, and my
accidental splendour bores me all the rest of the
time I have to dwell with it. No, the sort of
guest-chamber which I love to occupy in the
country is as simple as simple can be, and not so

crowded with furniture, but that a little space is
left here and there where a box can be placed
without its intruding itself as a nuisance for which
one feels constantly impelled to apologise. If I
am so fortunate as to find in a corner of my room
a little frame, about two feet high made by the

FIG. 31.

village carpenter, or the big boys of the house-
hold, for this box to stand on, then, indeed, I
know what luxury means. You have your box
so much more under your control if it is raised
a little from the floor, and it is ever so much
easier to pack and unpack. The taste and charac-
teristics of the owners of the house, which you may
be sure is to be found in all their surroundings,

is never more apparent than in the spare room. Sometimes your hostess tries to make you happy with looking-glasses, and I have shudderingly dwelt in a room with five large mirrors and sundry smaller ones; or else you are abashed to find how many gowns there is space for, and how few you have brought.   But this extreme is better than the other: I have had to keep my draperies on all the available chairs in the room because I was afraid to open and shut the diminutive drawers of an exquisite, aged coffre which was provided for their reception.   Beautiful as was this article of furniture, I would gladly have changed it for the commonest deal chest of drawers, long before the week was out.   In spare rooms, as in all other rooms, money is not everything.   It will not always buy taste, nor even comfort.   Doubtless many of my readers who may happen to have led as varied a life as mine has been, will agree with me in the assertion, that as far as actual *comfort* goes, they have often possessed it in a greater degree under a very humble roof-tree, than beneath many a more splendid shelter.   Everybody has their "little ways" (some of them very tiresome and odd, I admit), and there are splendid spare-rooms in which apparently no margin has been left, no indulgence shown, for any little individualities.

B. R.   I

I should not be an Englishwoman writing to other Englishwomen if I did not take it for granted that we all desire most ardently that our guests should be thoroughly comfortable in their own rooms as well as happy in our society, and so I venture to suggest that visitors should not be fettered by too many rules, that, however homely the plenishing of the guest-chamber must needs be, it should never lack a few fresh flowers, a place to write (Fig. 31), pen and ink, a tiny table which can be moved about at pleasure, a dark blind for the window, and such trifles which often make the difference between comfort and discomfort, between a homelike feeling directly one arrives, and the incessant consciousness of being " on a visit."

But with regard to spare rooms in a town house, what advice can be given beyond and except that horrid "don't"? Especially true is this in London. No one has the least idea how many affectionate relations he possesses until he has an empty bedroom in a London house. It would almost appear as if such things as hotels and lodgings had ceased to exist, so incessant, so importunate are the entreaties to be "put up" for a couple of nights. And let me say here that visitors will prove much more of a tax in London than they ever are in the country. For rural visitors

scarcely ever seem to realise or comprehend how
methodically mapped out is the life of a professional man living in London, how precious
are to him the quiet early hours which they insist
upon leaving behind them in the solitude of the
country. Speaking as a London hostess, I may
conscientiously assert that the guests who have
kept me up latest at night, who have voted break-
fast at 9.30 unreasonably early (without consider-
ing it was a whole hour later than our usual time)
have been those people who ordinarily led the
quietest and most clock-work existence in their
country home. I will say nothing here of the impossibility of inducing them to regard distance or
cab-hire as presenting any objection worth consideration in their incessant hunt after the bargains
erroneously supposed by them to be obtainable in
every shop. I have been scolded roundly by
country visitors for keeping early hours and leading
a quiet life in London, and I have never suc-
ceeded in impressing on them that in order to
get through a great deal of hard work, both my
husband and I found it necessary to do both.

To a professional man, with a small income,
the institution of a spare room may be regarded
as an income tax of several shillings in the pound
It is even worse than that; it means being forced
to take in a succession of lodgers who don't pay,

who are generally amazingly inconsiderate and *exigeante,* and who expect to be amused and advised, chaperoned and married, and even nursed and buried. It is inconceivable upon what slender grounds, or for what far-fetched reasons, your distant acquaintance, or your—compared to yourself —rich relation, will unhesitatingly demand your hospitality. And oh, my unknown friends, how often are we tempted to say yes to the well-to-do relation who asks the question of us, and to find an excuse to shut out the poor one who really needs it ? Ah how often ?

It is really a trial to be unable to receive one's nearest kith and kin, one's sailor brother or sister home from India, because "we have no spare room," yet that very beginning, natural and delightful as it is, cheerfully and laughingly borne as the little privations it entails may be, is often the beginning of a stream of self-invited guests who literally worry us, if they don't exactly "eat us," out of house and home.

THE END.

LONDON: R. CLAY, SONS, AND TAYLOR, BREAD STREET HILL.